Jeff Bezos

The Life, Lessons & Rules for Success

Influential Individuals

Table of Contents

Introduction

He knocked Bill Gates from the coveted spot of 'richest man in the world' in October 2017 and has held that position ever since. In 2018 alone, his wealth as of June has grown by almost $40 billion dollars. He founded the world's largest online retailer, and now wants to make it possible for humans to colonize space.

In short, Jeff Bezos is the man.

In this book we take a look at the life of Jeff Bezos. From humble beginnings in Albuquerque to present day CEO of Amazon. The book takes a look at the inspirations and influences that make Jeff Bezos the man he is today, and his approach towards life that has ensured the success he is now known for. The aim of this book is to not only give you a glimpse into the life of the world's richest man, but to also inspire and teach you some of the success principles that have guided Jeff Bezos so far.

Ready to learn from the richest man ever? Let's dive in.

Chapter One: Little Genius from Albuquerque

"If you double the number of experiments you do per year you're going to double your inventiveness." –
Jeff Bezos

In July 2017, American Entrepreneur Jeff Bezos surpassed Bill Gates to become the richest man in the world, with a net worth of $141 billion. The only person to ever cross the $100 billion mark is Bill Gates, whose net worth crossed the mark briefly back in 1999 following a bump in Microsoft stock. Jeff Bezos is known the world throughout. He is the founder and CEO of Amazon.com, the world's online retailing giant. Bezos is also the founder of Blue Origin, a space flight company he founded back in 2000 with the aim of commercializing space. Add to that the The Washington Post, which he bought back in 2013 for a whopping 250 million dollars.

To many people, Jeff Bezos is a highly intelligent and highly motivated billionaire who will stop at nothing to push the limits of technology and business. However, Bezos has not always been the billionaire the world knows today. Where did Jeff come from and how did he turn a seemingly crazy idea into the world's ecommerce giant? The story starts in the city of Albuquerque, deep in the deserts of New Mexico.

The Amazon CEO was born in Albuquerque, New Mexico on the 12th of January in 1964, as Jeffrey Preston Jorgensen to parents Jacklyn and Ted Jorgensen. At the time of his birth, Jeff's mother, Jacklyn, was only 17 years old. His father, Ted, was a unicyclist, a bicycle shop owner and a member of a group known as the Unicycle Wranglers who specialized in making performances in county circuses and fairs. A short while after Jeff's birth, his parents' marriage hit the rocks, forcing Jacklyn and Ted to separate before Jeff's second birthday. After the separation, Jeff's biological father entirely forgot about his young family, and only came to know of Jeff's billionaire status when being interviewed by an author who was writing a book about Jeff.

A few years after her first marriage broke down, Jeff's mother met and married a Cuban immigrant by the name Mike Bezos. Shortly after their marriage, Mike Bezos adopted Jeff as his legal son, and Jeff changed his surname to Bezos. Mike, real name Miguel Bezos, was born in the city of Santiago de Cuba in Cuba. Due to the tense political climate in Cuba at the time, Mike Bezos escaped to the United States at the age of 16, leaving his parents behind in Cuba. After moving to the United States, Mike managed to get a scholarship at the University of Albuquerque. Shortly after marrying Jeff's mother he gained employment at Exxon as an engineer, and the family moved to Houston.

Mike Bezos was a man of great discipline, drive and ambition. He managed to pay his way through college by working small odd jobs here and there. Much of this discipline, drive and ambition rubbed off on young Jeff, and has been instrumental to inspiring his work ethic. Another person who had a huge influence in young Jeff's life is his maternal grandfather, Lawrence Preston Guise. He was a Texan rancher, with a huge 25,000-acre ranch in Cotulla where young Jeff spent a lot of his summers. Lawrence had also worked in the U.S Atomic Energy Commission as a regional director. With a grandfather who was widely knowledgeable in the sciences and a father who worked as an engineer, it is no wonder that Jeff developed a love for mathematics and science at a young age. Jeff's intelligence and his inventive and experimental behavior started showing at a very young age. At the age of three, feeling that he was too grown-up to sleep in a baby crib instead of a real bed, Jeff used a screwdriver to dismantle his crib. At the age of five, Jeff watched on their black and white TV as the Apollo II made a landing on the moon. This was the beginning of his lifelong fascination with space, a fascination that would lead to the creation of Blue Origin. Jeff attended Royal Oaks Elementary School in Houston, where he was enrolled in a special program known as the Vanguard Program. The program was meant to encourage creative and out of the box thinking among students. In elementary school, Jeff showed an extraordinary level of intelligence and competitiveness. He was even featured in *Turning on Bright Minds: A Parent Looks at Gifted Education in Texas*, a book where the author described Jeff as a friendly but serious student who was not particularly gifted at leadership.

While in sixth grade at Royal Oaks, Jeff developed a survey to evaluate the school's teachers, not based on popularity, but rather based on how well they taught. At the age of twelve, Jeff saw a toy named the infinity cube at a store. The infinity cube was a battery powered toy that used rotating mirrors to create the illusion of an endless tunnel. Unable to afford the toy, which cost $22.00, Jeff went home and created his own version of the infinity cube. He bragged that his was cheaper than the original version he saw at the store.

The behavior of tinkering with and creating became a habit. He would sit in his bedroom creating his own robots and other similar projects. Over the years Mike and Jackie had two more children. Once they were old enough, they would go into Jeff's bedroom to see his amazing creations. Unhappy with this and wanting privacy, Jeff created an alarm system for his bedroom door to warn him when his half-siblings were going into his bedroom. At one point, the clutter in his room became so much that his parents asked him to make the family garage his workshop. Ironically, Jeff would also launch Amazon from a garage.

After several years, Jeff's step dad got a job transfer, forcing the family to move to Miami, Florida. After moving to Florida, Jeff transferred to the Palmetto Senior High School. During his time at Palmetto, Jeff once again showed his academic excellence. It was also at Palmetto that he discovered his love for computers. In 1982, he was invited to the Student Science Training Program, which was held at the University of Florida. Jeff went on to win the Silver Knight Award at the training program. Jeff was also popular in school. In his senior year, he was elected class president and valedictorian. Jeff Bezos graduated from Palmetto as a National Merit Scholar, earning himself a spot at Princeton University.

It was while at Palmetto that Bezos had his first encounter with retail and entrepreneurship. During one of his summer breaks, he worked as a fry cook at McDonald's, flipping burgers, scrambling eggs and making fries in response to the sound of buzzers. Bezos truly hated his time at McDonald's. In order to avoid working as a fry cook at McDonald's during the next summer break, Bezos and his then girlfriend Uschi Werner came up with his first entrepreneurial venture, which he named DREAM Institute. DREAM Institute was a summer education camp for younger kids in fourth, fifth and sixth grade. The term DREAM was an acronym for Directed REAsoning Methods. Jeff's DREAM Institute focused on science and literature. As part of the program, students were required to read a number of books, including *David Copperfield, Stranger in a Strange Land, Gulliver's Travels, Black Beauty, The Once and Future King, The Lord of the Rings, Treasure Island* and *Watership Down*. The science part of the program focused on topics such as space colonies and interstellar travel, fossil fuels and fusion, and TV and advertising. The DREAM Institute, which charged each student $600, managed to attract six signups, two of whom were Jeff's siblings. From his days in Palmetto Senior High School, Jeff had developed an admiration for Stephen Hawking. Therefore, when he enrolled at Princeton University, he intended to study physics, following the footsteps of Stephen Hawking. After enrolling into the physics program for a short while, Jeff gave up. He found that the program did not live up to his expectations. Rekindling his love for computers, Jeff transferred to a double major in computer science and electronics. During his time at Princeton, Jeff developed several software programs. He also became the president for Princeton's chapter of the Students for the Exploration and Development of Space. Bezos graduated from Princeton summa cum laude, with dual degrees in Computer Science and Electrical Engineering. He also garnered membership to honor societies Tau Beta Pi and Phi Beta Kappa.

Chapter Two: Early Career

"If we think long term we can accomplish things that we wouldn't otherwise accomplish. Time horizons matter. They matter a lot." – Jeff Bezos

---

Jeff Bezos did not launch Amazon immediately after leaving Princeton. He spent the majority of his 20's job hopping, the same way many millenials are spending their 20's today. On graduating from Princeton University in 1987, Bezos received job offers from huge companies such as Bell Labs, Intel, Andersen Consulting, and several others. Bezos turned them all down. Instead, he went to work for a fiber optic startup known as Fitel after answering an ad in *The Daily Princetonian* that was looking for the best computer science graduates from Princeton. Bezos was the 11th employee to be hired by Fitel, whose aim was to create an international telecommunications network to allow trading firms an easy and secure process for cross-border equity transactions.

Bezos started out life at Fitel as a code debugger. However, after demonstrating his excellence at the role, he was quickly promoted to the head of development and director of customer service. According to Graciela Chichilnisky, one of Fitel's co-founders, Bezos was a capable and upbeat employee who was highly devoted to his work, without caring what other people thought of him. Bezos stayed at Fitel for about two years, a period during which he worked tirelessly in trying to get the startup off the ground. The startup failed to make any reasonable growth, and in 1988, Bezos left Fitel and moved to Bankers Trust as a product manager. Bankers Trust is now part of Deutsche Bank.

After joining Bankers Trust, Bezos again received a series of promotions and soon became vice president. However, during his time at Bankers Trust, Bezos grew frustrated by the fact that institutions in the financial sector seemed reluctant to challenge the status quo. Bezos began thinking about starting his own business. In 1989, working on his spare time, he partnered with Halsey Minor – who was employed by Merrill Lynch – to start their own venture that would send customized newsletters to subscribers via fax. However, Merrill Lynch, which had promised to fund the venture, withdrew its support, leading to the collapse of the young venture. Halsey Minor would later leave Merrill Lynch to found CNET.

After two years at Bankers Trust, Bezos became bored with the financial sector. He started distributing his resume to recruiters with the aim of making a transfer from the financial sector to technology, a field that he felt held his real passion. Bezos believed computer automation was poised to revolutionize the business environment. Despite his intent to leave the financial sector, one headhunter managed to convince Bezos to take up a job at a two-and-a-half-year-old hedge fund known as D.E. Shaw & Co, referred to as DESCO by its employees. Despite being in financial services, DESCO was not an ordinary financial company.

DESCO was a quantitative hedge fund that had been started by David E. Shaw in 1988. Before forming DESCO, Shaw had been working as a computer science professor at Columbia University. DESCO was a financial firm that was focused on using complex mathematical formulas and computers to identify and take advantage of anomalous patterns in international financial markets. For instance, in situations where the same stocks had different prices in different countries or continents, the computer scientists at DESCO would come up with software programs to execute trades while taking advantage of these differences.

DESCO was different from conventional Wall Street firms in a number of ways. First and foremost, the firm did not employ financiers. Instead, David Shaw hired scientists and mathematicians. He searched for employees with extraordinary backgrounds, excellent academic performance and a dollop of social cluelessness. Shaw's aim was to turn DESCO into an iconic Wall Street firm by applying the capabilities of computers and technology to the financial sector in a scientific way. In addition, DESCO did not have any of the uncalled for formalities that were a natural part of other Wall Street firms. DESCO actually looked more like a Silicon Valley startup than a financial firm. DESCO employees were free to wear khakis and jeans instead of suits and ties. DESCO also applied the flat hierarchical structure that is characteristic of Silicon Valley startups. Despite the flat hierarchy, DESCO had a way of keeping their trading formulas secret from other Silicon Valley firms.

When Bezos joined DESCO, he immediately clicked with Shaw. Bezos actually considered Shaw to be a workplace soul mate. The fact that both of them were computer scientists also made it easier for them to get along. Just like in the previous companies he had worked at, Bezos rapidly moved up the ranks at DESCO. By 1992, two years after joining DESCO, Bezos had become a vice president at only 28, making him the youngest ever employee to become vice president at DESCO. Within four years of joining the hedge fund, Bezos had risen to the rank of senior vice president. There were only three other senior vice presidents.

While working at DESCO, Bezos showed many of the idiosyncratic characteristics that he has come to be known for. As throughout his life, he was always very disciplined and thorough with his work. At all times he carried a notebook where he kept a record of his ideas to prevent them escaping his memory. He was also very open minded. He had no trouble ditching old ways of doing things if he found a better method of achieving results.

From childhood to his current tenure as the CEO of Amazon, Bezos has always been obsessed with data. Most of his decisions and actions are based on a careful analysis of processes and data. This obsession with data and being analytical applies even to his personal life. While working at DESCO, he decided that it was the right time for him to start searching for a girlfriend. He did not want just any type of girlfriend. He wanted his potential lifetime mate to be smart and resourceful, or what he referred to as n+ women. To help him find a partner, Bezos started using a systematic approach in order to increase his 'women flow'. Women flow was a play on the phrase 'deal flow', which is a phrase for a Wall Street technique used to regulate the number of new deals they take in. Convinced that it would help him get exposed to n+

women, Bezos even went ahead to take ballroom dance classes.

Unfortunately, his systematic approach to dating did not help in his search for a girlfriend. However, the stringent recruitment requirements and measures applied attracted women with the kind of smarts and resourcefulness that Bezos was looking for in a woman. MacKenzie Tuttle, who would become the future MacKenzie Bezos, was an English major who had graduated from Princeton. After a stint working as an assistant to author Toni Morrison, MacKenzie joined DESCO as an administrative assistant, and shortly after, started working directly under Bezos. The two fell in love and started dating. After three months of dating, Bezos and MacKenzie were engaged, and then married three months later in 1993.

During his time at DESCO, Bezos was a workaholic. He even had a sleeping bag in his office in case he needed to spend a night at the office. The sleeping bag was rarely used, since most of his time at the office was spent working. By this time, DESCO had already started dabbling into the developing world of the internet. DESCO had already registered its URL in 1992, making it among the very first Wall Street firms to do so. Goldman Sachs registered its URL in 1995, while Morgan Stanley registered theirs in 1996. In 1993, Bezos was put in charge of finding any new business opportunities that the internet presented for DESCO.

Bezos had some experience with the internet during his school days at Princeton. However, he had not considered any commercial applications of the technology before coming to DESCO. Each week, Bezos and Shaw held brainstorming sessions to find ideas on how DESCO could take advantage of the internet to grow its business. Bezos would then research the ideas they came up with to determine their feasibility. While researching on the internet one day, Bezos came across the statistic that the usage of the internet was growing at a rate of 2300 percent every month, causing a light bulb moment.

To Bezos, such an amount of growth was incredible and represented a huge opportunity. Immediately he set out to explore the feasibility of starting an online business. After brainstorming for ideas of what to sell over the internet and creating a list of 20 possible products, he came to the conclusion that books were the most logical thing to sell over the internet. To Bezos, it was impossible for a physical bookstore to stock a comprehensive inventory of print books. Instead, most bookstores turned to book distributors in case a customer asked for a book that was not in stock. In addition, the top two book distributors in the country already had exhaustive electronic catalogues of the books they had in stock. Bezos surmised that if he had a central database of an exhaustive catalogue of books from which customers could order and buy books, then he could easily take much of the business from physical bookstores.

After concluding that the prospect of selling books on the internet presented a very exciting opportunity, Bezos approached Shaw with his idea. Shaw did not see any potential in the idea, and was not ready to devote the firm's resources to the idea. Bezos, on the other hand, was still convinced that the internet was the next frontier of business. Unable to convince Shaw to give priority to his idea, Bezos announced to Shaw that he would be leaving DESCO to go and start his own internet company. Shaw tried his best to persuade Bezos to remain at DESCO. Taking a walk in Central Park, Shaw had a talk with Bezos, asking him to consider the implications of the decision he was about to make. By leaving, not only would Bezos be leaving behind a financially secure position, but also a chance to play a crucial role at DESCO. At one point, Shaw even made it clear to Bezos that DESCO would probably become a competitor to his new company. Jeff, however, had made his decision, and no one could change his mind.

Chapter Three: Building The World's Ecommerce Giant

"People don't have any idea yet how impactful the internet is going to be and that this is still Day 1 in such a big way."
– Jeff Bezos

By 1994, Jeff Bezos was already successful by ordinary standards. He was the senior vice president at DESCO, the youngest person to ever hold that position. As senior vice president, he was already earning a six figure income. Having already shown his worth, and with his close relationship with David Shaw, it was inevitable that Bezos would rise even further at DESCO. It is therefore no surprise that Shaw tried to dissuade him from leaving DESCO. However, Bezos had been bitten by the entrepreneurial bug. Nothing could keep him from giving his idea a shot. At the time, the internet was still a relatively new phenomenon. Bezos was taking a huge risk, with no certainty that his gamble would pay off.

Before leaving DESCO, Jeff Bezos was well aware of the consequences of the decision he was about to make. However, the 2300% figure kept ringing in his head. To help him make the right decision, Bezos came up with what he referred to as the "regret minimization framework". He tried to imagine the things that he would regret when he was eighty years of age. It was unlikely that he would regret leaving a job at a Wall Street firm at the age of 30. He was young, intelligent and could recover if things were to go wrong. If the internet exploded and other people took advantage of the opportunities it presented, he would live with regrets about missing the chance when he had it. With this line of thought, leaving DESCO was an easy decision for Bezos.

With the decision made, Bezos and his wife MacKenzie set out on the now famous drive to Seattle to put his plan into action. Bezos settled on Seattle as the ideal location to launch his startup for two major reasons. Firstly, Seattle would give Bezos access to a huge pool of high-tech talent that would be crucial in helping him get his new startup off the ground. Second and most important, Seattle was in close proximity to one of the warehouses owned by Ingram, one of the country's two leading book distributors. Being near the warehouse made it easier for Bezos to have more control over the shipping process during Amazon's foundation stage. The drive to Seattle was a busy one for Bezos. As his wife drove, Bezos was busy creating a business plan on his laptop and making calls to possible investors.

Before heading out to Seattle, Bezos had already spent some time trying to lay the foundation for his new company. He held 60 meetings trying to convince family members and friends to put in roughly $50,000 each into his idea. At the time, the idea of an online bookshop seemed quite crazy, and as you can bet, many of those he spoke to did not recognize the potential to his idea. Just like his former employer David Shaw. Of the 60 people he spoke to, 38 of them rejected the opportunity to invest in Bezos' idea, thereby missing a chance to be part of Amazon's history. The other 22 who invested in the 'Amazon thing' that Bezos couldn't stop talking about – including Bezos' parents and two siblings – were given about 1% of Amazon's stock on average.

At today's market price for Amazon stocks, the 1% was enough to make each of them a billionaire, providing of course they held on to all their stock. Jeff's parents Mike and Jacklyn, who invested about $300,000 into the company, got about 6% of Amazon stock. At the time, Mike Bezos did not even know what the internet was. Therefore, by putting his money into Amazon, he was not betting on the company or the opportunities presented by the internet, but rather on his adopted son.

Other than searching for investors for his new company, Bezos had also started looking for employees for Amazon. Even before leaving DESCO, Bezos had made a trip to California to meet up with three talented programmers he'd heard about from a DESCO partner. After talks over breakfast, Bezos was able to convince a programmer named Shel Kaphan to become Amazon's first employee. Convincing Kaphan to work for Amazon was no small task. Despite being a very talented programmer, Kaphan had earned himself a reputation as a great pessimist. Kaphan believed that most tech companies' systems were always a small mistake away from failure. Kaphan's pessimism was not unfounded. He had worked for several tech startups that had ended up in failure. However, his pessimism made him a great programmer because he was always looking for ways to improve systems to prevent the ever impending failure he had come to expect. Before meeting Bezos, Kaphan had just left Kaleida Labs, an Apple spin-off that was about to tank. Having seen so many tech startups going belly up, it was a wonder Bezos was able to convince Kaphan to work on a project that was just an idea in Bezos' mind. Kaphan would play such an important role in Amazon's early days that at one point, Bezos termed him as the "...most important person ever in the history of Amazon."

Though Kaphan was never listed as an Amazon co-founder, he was a crucial part of Amazon since the idea stage.

With some of the money he had raised from investors, Bezos rented a house in the Bellevue suburb of Seattle and converted the cramped, poorly insulated garage into the headquarters of his new company. He was essentially going back to his childhood setting of using a garage to conduct experiments. The garage contained a pot bellied stove at the center of the room and three Sun SPARC stations. The garage looked a mess, with extension cords running all over the place. Later, in a bid to create more space within the garage, the stove was done away with and a set of ceramic space heaters were brought in to take its place.

Bezos went out and hired two more employees to help him get his new company off the ground. The second employee to be hired by Amazon was Paul Barton Davis. Davis came to Amazon even before the company had launched its website. Together with Kaphan, they played a huge role in helping bring Bezos' vision to life. Before joining Amazon, Davis' former colleagues at the University of Washington were so concerned that the new company Davis was joining would fail, that they collected a few dollars in a coffee can and gave them to Davis as donations in case Amazon went belly up. Bezos also hired another employee named Lovejoy, who had been a former colleague at DESCO.

This team of three employees, plus Jeff Bezos and his wife MacKenzie, comprised the initial group that kick started Amazon; designing, prototyping and testing the website. Kaphan would stay with the company until Bezos promoted him to CTO after hiring two new tech managers. Feeling that he could not make any real impact in the company from his new position, Kaphan, who loved to get his hands dirty with the actual coding, decided to leave Amazon. Davis would also leave the company after about two years.

When Bezos came up with the idea of selling books over the internet, he did not intend to name his company Amazon. Instead, he wanted to name it Cadabra, which sounded magical to him. Cadabra was derived from the magical term abracadabra. However, when he called his lawyer, Todd Tarbert, asking him to register the name for him, Todd misheard the name as Cadaver. He was appalled that Bezos wanted to name his company Cadaver, and he asked Bezos to reconsider the name. Bezos then toyed with the idea of naming his virtual business 'Relentless', but he later decided to name it Amazon, after South America's largest river. However, the name 'Relentless' still stuck with Bezos, and he eventually ended up buying the domain. Today, if you visit www.relentless.com, you will be redirected to Amazon.com.

For around a year after moving to Seattle, Bezos and his crew worked on Amazon from his garage, creating a user-friendly interface for the website and learning how to source books from different distributors. Like many other billionaires, such as the legendary Steve Jobs, Bezos is a true marketing visionary. From the very beginning, he was focused on making Amazon as customer centric as possible. Apart from creating a user-friendly interface that made the process of virtual shopping as easy as possible, Bezos also wanted Amazon to have the feel of a virtual community for shoppers. In order to achieve this feeling of community, Bezos came up with several innovative features, such as making it possible for customers to give book reviews, as well as another feature that would make book recommendations to customers based on other books they had purchased previously. These two features have grown to become a crucial part of modern day ecommerce.

After a year of working on the virtual bookstore, Bezos reached out to over 300 friends and acquaintances, asking them to test the site. Bezos and his team had done an amazing job, and the code worked as they had envisioned across multiple computer platforms. After some rigorous testing, Amazon.com finally opened its doors to the public in July 1995. With over a million book titles available, the tagline for the newly launched virtual bookstore was the 'Earth's Biggest Bookstore'. Surprisingly, Bezos did not launch Amazon.com with any pomp or fanfare. There was no press release to announce that Amazon.com was now live. Instead, Bezos asked his beta testers to spread the word about the new site. Despite the lack of press coverage, word about the new virtual bookstore spread like wildfire. The huge catalogue of book titles, the ease of use and exemplary customer service provided by Amazon greatly captivated users. Internet users started talking about the new online book store on internet forums, and word immediately got to internet newsgroups. A few days after launch, Amazon sold a book about artificial intelligence, its first book sale. Within the first month, Amazon had made sales in all the 50 states as well as in 45 foreign countries. Within two months, sales had grown to about $20,000 each week. During the first few days after launch, the site was wired such that a bell would sound every time a purchase was made. Amazon staff would then rush to the computers to see if anyone among them knew the customer. However, within a few weeks, the bell was sounding so many times that they had to turn it off. During the first few days after launch, Amazon hit its first challenge. Most book distributors only sold to retailers who wanted ten or more books with each order. However, since it was still in its early stages, Amazon did not need such a huge inventory. Fortunately, Bezos discovered a loophole in the distributors' order policies. While retailers had to order 10 or more books, it was a requirement that the retailer had to receive as many books. Therefore, Bezos would ask his team to order the book a customer wanted, and nine copies of a book about lichens that they had discovered was never in stock. Amazon would therefore receive the only one book that they needed to mail to their customer.

With sales streaming in steadily, Bezos did not rest on his laurels. Instead, he continued making improvements to the site. The site soon incorporated features such as email order verification and one-click shopping, features that were unknown before then. By September of the following year, Amazon had grown to a staff of about 100 employees. Orders were still streaming in, earning the company over $15.7 million in sales revenue. Without the constraints of a brick and mortar book store, Amazon continued expanding its catalogue. By 1997, Amazon had over 2.5 million titles available on the site. The user base grew to over 1.5 million customers across over one hundred and fifty countries. In 1997, Amazon made sales of over $148 million. Within three years, the company would grow to over 3,000 employees and sales of over $610 million.

The business was growing faster than anyone had expected, including Bezos himself. On the 15th of May, 1997, Amazon went public, with a market cap of about $438 million and a stock price of $18 per share. At a time when most startups of the dotcom era were collapsing, skeptics doubted whether Amazon would survive the burst of the dotcom bubble. However, Amazon proved its critics wrong. By 1999, its market cap had grown bigger than the combined market share of its two biggest competitors.

Ever since Amazon's earliest days, Bezos projected his workaholic tendencies on his employees. Bezos had no concern for the notion of a work-life balance, and he expected the same of Amazon employees. Amazon employees were expected to clock a minimum of 60 hours each week. One of the earliest employees at Amazon worked so hard over an 8-month period – riding his bicycle to work early in the morning and back home late at night – that he forgot about his car, which he had parked down the street near his apartment. With his early mornings and late nights, he never got around to reading his mail. When he finally found the time to go through his mail, he found several parking tickets, a tow notice, a couple of warnings from the towing company, and a final notice about his car being sold off at an auction.

The rapid growth that Amazon was experiencing soon

attracted the attention of Barnes & Noble, who had been the book retailing giants before the emergence of Amazon. In a bid to take advantage of the internet and reclaim part of the market share that Amazon had taken from them, they quickly built their own virtual bookstore, www.barnesandnoble.com. In a bid to unsettle Amazon from the title of the 'Earth's Biggest Bookstore', they launched an audacious marketing campaign with the claim that their book inventory was twice as big as that of Amazon. Unfortunately for them, Bezos was already miles ahead, both in market share and in strategy. Shortly after Barnes & Noble launched their campaign, Bezos introduced a new CD's category to Amazon's offerings. The tagline 'Earth's Biggest Bookstore' was replaced by 'Books, Music and More'. In so doing, Bezos rendered Barnes & Noble's offence strategy useless, leaving them clutching at a ghost.

The skyrocketing share price of Amazon stock in 1999 created a number of billionaires, including Bezos and his parents. Bezos approached his rapidly growing wealth with a modesty that seems so common within the tech industry, yet so unnatural among outsiders. In Silicon Valley, it is not uncommon to find young millionaires in their twenties who use public transport and hole up in their parent's spare bedroom, despite all their wealth. The same happened with

Bezos. Even after he had attained billionaire status, very little about his lifestyle changed. Despite being worth over $9 billion in 1999, Bezos and his wife still lived in the same one bedroom Seattle apartment they had moved into when launching Amazon in 1994. It would take another year before he bought their $10 million Lake Washington mansion, and another several years before he bought the string of properties he owns currently, including a series of properties on Lake Washington, four apartments in Manhattan's Central Park West worth over $40 million, two homes in Beverly Hills worth a combined $37+ million, a 300 acre Texas ranch and a former Washington DC museum that he paid over $23 million for.

At one time, when teased on TV about making it to the list of the Forbes 400 wealthiest Americans, Bezos played down the achievement, saying that the only difference his wealth made was that he no longer looked at menu prices before making his order. He was also quick to emphasize that the most important thing for him to keep in mind was that it was crucial for the company to keep serving its customers well, since for himself and other Amazon investors, their wealth only existed on paper. Poor performance by the company would negatively affect their wealth.

However, like other tech billionaires, Bezos does not shy away from splurging huge amounts of money to have a fantastic time with friends. In August 1999, Bezos organized the 'Shelebration', a surprise four-day trip to Maui to celebrate Shel Kaphan's fourth anniversary as a member of the Amazon team. During the trip, Bezos chartered a jet to ferry himself and his wife, Kaphan, and several other Amazon employees and their spouses to Maui. He chartered another jet to fly a group of Kaphan's old friends from San Jose to Maui.

From the very start Bezos was more concerned about getting a huge market share, even if that came at the expense of profits. In his business plan for Amazon, Bezos did not expect to make profits for the first five years. The aim was to first build a customer centric business that everyone turned to when they needed to buy something online. His gamble paid off. As other companies evaporated with the burst of the dotcom bubble, Amazon was making huge profits. Bezos continually restructured the company and expanded into other categories. After the introduction of CD's went through successfully, Bezos introduced a temporary gift section to Amazon.com during the Christmas of 1998, allowing customers to purchase toys and games. Bezos also started the trial of a program that was named 'Shop the Web', through which Amazon would earn affiliate commissions for sending customers to other online retailers that were not deemed as competitors of

Amazon. In 1999 January, Amazon bought a share of Drugstore.com in a bid to tap into the huge US pharmacy market.

When auction sites like eBay and uBID came onto scene, Bezos did not want to get left behind as other people made money through online auctions. In June 1999, Amazon entered into a partnership with Sotheby's Holdings Inc. Shortly after, Amazon launched its own online auction site, www.sothebys.amazon.com. However, the online auction site did not pick up, forcing Bezos to abandon it. Shortly after, Amazon introduced a consumer electronics section to Amazon.com. By this time, Bezos was focused on transforming Amazon from selling 'Books, Music and More' into 'The Everything Store'. Three years later, in October 2002, Amazon added clothing to its offerings by getting into partnerships with several clothing retailers, such as Nordstrom, The Gap and Land's End. In 2006, Bezos steered Amazon into the on-demand video industry with the launch of Amazon Unbox on Tivo, which later changed its name to Amazon Instant Video.

At the turn of the millennium, Amazon also realized that it had an unexploited technology gold mine. Amazon had already invested in very strong servers to host its online shop. The company figured out that some of this server space could be leased off to other people trying to build online businesses, giving birth to Amazon Web Services. At the very beginning, Amazon Web Services did not attract a huge number of customers. However, the launch of the Apple iPhone created a new mobile app industry. With the simplicity and affordability of Amazon Web Services, many of these apps, including Candy Crush and Tinder began using Amazon Web Services as the backbone of their services. As the mobile app industry grew, so did Amazon Web Services. Though the service was facing competition from Google, Alibaba, IBM and Microsoft, it still managed to hold its position as a dominant force in cloud computing. Today, Amazon is setting itself up to be a leader in the next technological evolution by allowing developers to build applications on top of its machine learning and voice computing platforms.

In 2005, Amazon introduced a new service known as Amazon Prime. This service required users to subscribe for an annual membership in exchange for free two-day shipping as well as discounts for one-day shipping on select items. Over time, Amazon introduced Amazon Video, a service that allows Amazon Prime members to stream some select TV programs and films at no extra cost. In 2011, Amazon made it possible for Amazon prime users to borrow some Kindle eBooks for free for up to one month. In 2014, Amazon introduced Prime

Music, giving users access to free music streaming. Later the same year, the company also introduced Prime Photos, giving users unlimited photo storage in their Amazon Drive accounts.

In 2007, convinced that the future of books was in eBooks rather than print books, Bezos launched the Kindle, a handheld e-reading device. One of the most revolutionary features of the Kindle was the use of e-ink, which made it possible for the device to make text appear like print, thereby allowing readers to read from the e-reader without experiencing eye strain as is the case with computer and TV screens. With the Kindle, readers could also adjust the font size of their e-reader, therefore making reading more comfortable. In addition, the Kindle e-reader had wireless connectivity, allowing customers to buy and read books on the move. The introduction of the Kindle increased Amazon's sales by about 38% and increased profits by more than 100%. While eBooks are priced way lower than hardcover books, thus lowering profits and royalties for authors and publishers, they increased the number of book sales. By mid-2010, Amazon had reached $2.38 billion in eBook and Kindle sales, and the retail giant started selling more eBooks than hardcover books.

The introduction of the Kindle e-reader helped Amazon amass

about 95% of the eBook market in the United States. The Kindle reigned supreme until the launch of the iPad tablet computer by Apple in 2010. To fight and retain Amazon's dominance, Bezos responded by adding new features to the Kindle and reducing its price. In 2011, Amazon launched a new device to compete with the Apple iPad. Dubbed the Kindle Fire, the new device was a fully-fledged tablet computer with a color touch screen. In 2012, Amazon launched the Kindle Paperwhite.

In 2013, Bezos paid $250 million to purchase the newspaper division of the Washington Post. Bezos bought the Washington Post with his own money, which means that Amazon does not own the Washington Post. As part of the deal, Bezos also bought several other smaller newspapers operating within Washington DC. The purchase changed the ownership of the Washington Post from the Graham Family for the first time in eight decades. While Bezos did not change the management of the Washington Post, he has had an influence on its operations. Since the change in ownership, the Washington Post has seen tremendous growth in unique visitors, to the point where it even attracted more visitors than the New York Times for the very first time.

Today, Amazon is banking on a new service known as Amazon Air Prime. This is an experimental service that intends to use unmanned aerial drones to make deliveries to customers in less than 30 minutes. The drones will only deliver packages weighing less than five pounds to customers within a 10-mile radius from an Amazon distribution center. Amazon has already started testing out drone deliveries in multiple locations.

While Amazon has seen rapid growth since its inception in 1994, everything has not been success after success for Jeff Bezos. Part of his success can be attributed to his approach to failure. Where other CEOs and companies are afraid of failure, Bezos does not really care. His indifference towards failure explains his experimental nature that has helped him disrupt the retail industry. To him, the only way to take bold bets is to experiment, and there is no way of predicting with certainty whether an experiment will work. It is by embracing failure that Bezos has been able to achieve success. In the course of building Amazon, Bezos has experienced a number of failures. For instance, in 2000, he invested over $60 million into a shampoo delivery service known as Kozmo.com, which died a short while after. The attempt to build an online auction site was another failure. In 2012, Bezos purchased LivingSocial and ended up losing about $175 million. Perhaps his most famous failure is the Fire Phone, which he launched in a bid to compete with the iPhone. The phone was a huge flop, to the extent that even a reduction of price to 99 cents was unable to save it.

Despite all the growth experienced by Amazon, the biggest winner in the Amazon story is Bezos himself. Today, Bezos owns 16% of Amazon stock. In July 2017, a bump in Amazon share price helped Bezos surpass Bill Gates briefly to become the richest person in the world, before falling back to second position. However, he regained the top position in October 2017, and has held it ever since. By July 2018, Bezos had a net worth of $141 billion, making him the richest person of all time.

Chapter Four: Blue Origin: Journey into Space

"Going to space is not something that we may choose to do; this is something we must do." – Jeff Bezos

---

The journey of growing Amazon from garage based startup into the world's largest online retail site did not deter Jeff Bezos from his childhood dream of colonizing space. At the age of 5, Bezos watched on his parents' black and white TV as Neil Armstrong and Buzz Aldrin became the first humans to set foot on the moon. Watching the moon landing was a moment of amazement and inspiration for young Bezos. He was convinced that the future of mankind was in space colonization, not just space exploration. During his graduation speech at Palmetto Senior High School, Bezos spoke of a time when millions of us would be living in space. This fascination with space also led him to become president of the Students for the Exploration and Development of Space during his time at Princeton.

This childhood dream of colonizing space has remained with Bezos throughout his life. Today, as the richest man in the world, he has everything he could want to start transforming his dream into reality. To achieve this momentous goal, unsurprisingly, Bezos is ready to channel all his wealth into space travel. Once again, he's willing to go all in. In 2000, he secretly founded Blue Origin, a space focused startup that has one goal: to make space travel cheap, routine and frequent. According to Bezos, Blue Origin is his most important venture, even more important than Amazon.

You might be wondering why he thinks Blue Origin is more crucial than the company that has made him the world's richest man. According to Bezos, humans are a species that are constantly seeking advancement. In our quest for advancement, we end up using more and more energy and resources. The human population is also constantly growing. If we confine ourselves to life on planet earth, it will get to a point where no further growth can be achieved. We will deplete the resources on earth and it will be impossible for planet earth to support the population. When we get to such a point, the only salvation for the human race will be to move to space.

Bezos envisions a point in time where millions of people will live and work in space. According to Bezos, space is ripe for colonization for a number of reasons. First and foremost, there are numerous natural resources in space. For instance, the moon - which is the first target in Bezos' sights – has massive ice deposits, which Bezos says can be converted into oxygen, water and fuel. The moon being a short distance away from earth makes it a prime target for space colonization. Also, Bezos believes that it will be easier to harness solar energy from space.

With an abundance of resources and energy, Bezos believes space colonies will become the industrial zones that support the earth. All the heavy industrial activities will be done in space, while earth will be zoned as a place for residential and light industrial use. Manufacturing will be done on the moon and on other planets with finished products sent down to earth. Without any heavy industrial activity on earth, it will become possible to prevent the environmental degradation that has become a huge concern over the last decade.

While Bezos ideas seem far-fetched, he is being realistic with the timelines. He is using the same long term vision he had when founding Amazon to anticipate problems that will plague earth in the future. His plans for space colonization are not meant to come true in the next five years. Not even ten. Instead, he knows that overpopulation and climate change might be a huge problem on earth in a hundred years to come, and therefore, he wants people to be prepared well in advance.

Bezos, through his company Blue Origin, has started preparing for that future when people will be going to and from space as they please. While Bezos was keen on keeping Blue Origin and its operations secretive, the company came into the limelight after NASA awarded it millions of dollars' worth of contracts. In 2004, Bezos spent a portion of his fortune to purchase a 30,000-acre piece of land in Texas to act as the testing and launching his rockets. He has since bought an additional 330,000 acres of land in the region.

Blue Origin has already built its first operational rocket, which is christened the New Shepard as a tribute to Alan Shepard, America's first astronaut. The New Shepard is designed to be a reusable rocket that can launch into space and land back on earth safely in readiness for another flight. According to Bezos, for people to go to space and come back as they please, there is need for reusable rockets that can handle several flights, instead of having to build a new rocket for every space expedition. Key to the New Shepard's ability to land back on earth is a ring situated near the top of the rocket that helps stabilize the rocket as it hurtles down towards earth at supersonic speeds. The New Shepard has been tested and proven to work. In 2015, Blue Origin launched this rocket to the edge of space and landed it back safely five times in a row, proving that Bezos is indeed onto something with the reusable rocket.

Blue Origin is already working on a second rocket, which they have named the New Glenn. Like the New Shepard, the New Glenn is also designed to be reusable. However, the New Glenn will be a massive rocket, with a lifting power 35 times more than that of the New Shepard. Bezos envisions that the New Glenn will one day be used to send 100 or more passengers into space. Bezos has already constructed a 750,000 square foot hangar in Cape Canaveral, Florida, where the New Glenn is being built, and from where it will be launched. He expects that the New Glenn will be ready to take its maiden flight by the year 2020.

To an ordinary person, Bezos' fascination with space might seem like a rich man's hobby. However, to Bezos, it is more than a hobby. Today, the European Space Agency is advocating for the creation of an International Moon Village, a permanent human presence on the surface of the moon that will serve as the headquarters for projects on the lunar surface as well as a stopover point for expeditions to Mars. Bezos knows that expeditions to the International Moon Village will need a cheap form of transport, and through Blue Origin, he is positioning himself for market dominance when this time comes. While other space entrepreneurs like Richard Branson and Elon Musk are focused on projects like space tourism and space colonization, Bezos is keeping his business interests more practical. Just like he did with Amazon, he is positioning Blue Origin to be the go-to Logistics Company for space travel.

Today, Bezos is already sinking a lot of money into Blue Origin. He has stated that he will liquidate $1 billion of Amazon stock every year and channel it to Blue Origin. Bezos might be losing money on Blue Origin, but he definitely knows what he is doing. For the first few years, Amazon did not post any profits, yet it made Bezos the richest man in the world two decades later. Similarly, Blue Origin might be losing money at the moment, but it might turn his wealth into a trillion dollar fortune three decades from today.

Chapter Five: 10 Success Principles to Live By

"Life's too short to hang out with people who aren't resourceful." – Jeff Bezos

---

Jeff Bezos knows what it takes to be successful. The convenience of online shopping that Bezos helped to evolve has become a major part of the modern world. Who knows, he might also be part of the team that makes it possible for us to make the moon, or some other planet, a permanent residence. All that Bezos has achieved thus far has been truly phenomenal and inspirational. While not everyone is aspiring to build the next Amazon or become a space entrepreneur, we can still learn from the principles he has followed throughout his life to fully unlock our own potential.

REGRET MINIMIZATION FRAMEWORK

When Bezos first had the idea of starting Amazon, he was already successful. He was earning a six figure salary as the senior vice president of DESCO, and he was poised to climb even higher up the corporate ladder. Therefore, it came as a surprise when he announced his plans to quit and start his own company. His former employer tried to dissuade him from leaving. On hearing his plans, his parents' first reaction was to ask him whether he knew what he was doing. Bezos himself knew he was making a very risky decision. However, he used the regret minimization framework to help him make the decision. Would he regret the decision to quit from DESCO when he looked back at his life at the age of 80? Very unlikely. If he quit and his new venture failed, he could always find employment again. However, if he failed to take the opportunity to try out his idea and his hunch turned out to be right, he would live a life of regret.

We always face the dilemma of choosing between the safe option and the riskier but more rewarding option. In such situations, using the risk minimization framework will help you make a better decision. If you are afraid of taking a risk, ask yourself this: Will the outcome matter in 5 years? What about 10 years from now? What about 30 or 50 years from now? If the outcome will not matter down the line, go ahead and take the plunge. Life will never be perfect, so the best thing is to live a life without too many regrets.

"The framework I found, which made the decision incredibly easy, was what I called — which only a nerd would call — a "regret minimization framework." So I wanted to project myself forward to age 80 and say, "Okay, now I'm looking back on my life. I want to have minimized the number of regrets I have." I knew that when I was 80 I was not going to regret having tried this. I was not going to regret trying to participate in this thing called the Internet that I thought was going to be a really big deal. I knew that if I failed I wouldn't regret that, but I knew the one thing I might regret is not ever having tried. I knew that that would haunt me every day, and so, when I thought about it that way it was an incredibly easy decision."

Bezos makes an important distinction between a decision you can live with and the potential for failure based on that decision. There's a huge difference between experiencing regret and experiencing a poor outcome. Failure is part of life so you can't expect every risk to pay off for you. At times you have to accept small regrets in order to avoid large ones. Have you minimized the number of regrets in your life?

GATHER THE RIGHT PEOPLE AROUND YOU

Bezos has always been careful about the people around him, not only at work, but also in his personal life. When starting Amazon, he went to Seattle because he knew this would give him access to the kind of talent he would need for his new venture. His hiring process at Amazon is very rigorous, influenced by the hiring practices he learnt at DESCO. This is because he wants to make sure that he has the right kind of people working for him. Even when choosing a potential life partner, he was very specific about the kind of woman he wanted to share his life with. He knew he wanted a smart and resourceful woman, and he even started taking ballroom dance classes because he thought they would increase his chances of meeting such a woman.

Just like Bezos, it is important to make sure that you surround yourself with the right kind of people. The people you work with and spend time around have a huge influence on your life. Therefore, if you want to live your best life and achieve your dreams, surround yourself with people who are likely to help you achieve that dream.

GRADATIM FEROCITER

Bezos explains that his motto is *gradatim ferociter*, which is Latin for "step-by-step courageously."

When starting Amazon, Bezos had a long term vision of becoming the world's biggest online retailer. He knew this would take time. He was ready to forego profits in the short term at the expense of building his brand. Once he started making profits, he reinvested them into Amazon. His efforts paid back decades later by making him the richest man on earth. Bezos is showing the same long term vision with Blue Origin, starting to find solutions for problems that will plague the earth a century from now, a time when he will not be alive. Bezos refers to long-term thinking as a key mindset, and has used this repeatedly at Amazon.

"What we're really focused on is thinking long-term, putting the customer at the center of our universe and inventing," Bezos explains in an interview with Four Peaks TV. "Those are the three big ideas to think long-term because a lot of invention doesn't work. When you're first creating something, whether it's a new business or a product, you have to invent.

If you're going to invent, it means you're going to experiment, and you'll have to think long-term."

If things don't initially go your way, it can be difficult not to panic and stay true to the course. Bezos offers this advice: Be straightforward and clear about how you're going to operate and what you want to get done from the beginning.

Bezos adds that you must be clear not only with yourself, but also with those around you. That way, he says, they can "self-select in."

Bezos understands the importance of looking into the future but also emphasizes that all things take time. Whenever a milestone is reached, it should be acknowledged. Amazon ensures congratulatory messages are sent to the employees when earned.

"Big things start small. The biggest oak starts from an acorn, you've got to be willing to let that acorn grow into a little sapling, and then finally into a small tree and then maybe one day it'll be a big business on its own. You can't skip steps. You have to put one foot in front of the other. Things take time. There are no shortcuts, but you want to do those steps with passion and ferocity."

This is the same approach you should have for your life. Instead of focusing on short term gains, think about the future. Have long term goals and then make short term plans that will help you achieve your long term goal.

MAKE YOUR OWN RULES

PowerPoint at meetings is standard practice for pretty much all businesses. Not Amazon. Bezos has a more unconventional approach as how to present and pitch ideas at meetings and presentations.

Employees are requested to write a roughly five-page narrative before the meeting. This is distributed to members upon arrival to read for the first 15-20 minutes of the meeting. Next, whoever is presenting takes questions about the idea. This is certainly a unique method for showcasing new ideas, Bezos as you would expect, has his reasons for this method. He believes this ensures the person carefully thinks through their idea before bringing it to his attention. Something a few bullet points on a PowerPoint does not achieve. He explains: "PowerPoint-style presentations somehow give permission to gloss over ideas, flatten out any sense of relative importance, and ignore the interconnectedness of ideas," he wrote in a 2004 memo explaining his decision to purge PowerPoint from Amazon.

Blue Origin president Meyerson was reluctant to engage in this practice. However, he relented. And now he admits to being a "complete convert."

FAILURE SHOULD NOT BE FEARED

When Bezos decided to leave DESCO to start Amazon, there was a very high chance that his new venture would fail. The internet was still a new phenomenon. No one had attained any massive success using the internet for business. Yet Bezos was willing to take the risk. He actually gave himself only a 30% chance of succeeding. Over the course of his life at Amazon, he has not been afraid to experiment with different products, even if experimentation presents a risk of failure. He tried to launch an auction site for Amazon, which failed. His efforts at launching the Fire Phone to compete with the iPhone also flopped. Failure has never held him back from trying new things.

In life, many people are held back from trying new things by the fear of failure. However, if you accept failure as a natural part of success, you are more likely to try new things, one of which might give you your lucky break. When it comes to luck, remember what Seneca said "Luck is what happens when preparation meets opportunity." Do not let your fear of failure hold you back from achieving your vision.

HARD PIVOT TOWARD THE WINNING IDEA

Bezos possesses the winning combination of taking educated risks through following the data. He is not afraid to change direction if that is what the data is telling him. Leaving his successful job as senior vice president of a hedge fund is a prime example of this. He saw the potential in his idea and had the courage to take a complete U-turn on his career. It's safe to say he made the right decision.

BE STUBBORN ABOUT YOUR VISION

It is not enough to simply have a vision; you also need to be stubborn about your vision. When Bezos decided that he would try his hand at building the world's largest online retail business, no one could dissuade him from doing it. To find funding for his idea, he talked to over 60 people, many of who told him his idea had no potential. No matter what they could not deter him from going for it. Before starting Blue Origin, Bezos had the vision of becoming a space entrepreneur at the age of five. He held fast onto that vision until he had enough money to act upon his idea.

This is a very important trait to live by. Once you create a vision for your life, follow it with determination. Don't let anything sidetrack you from your goal. Remember in as much as it is a good thing to be stubborn in your vision, do not be so fixated on the small details. If some part of your plan does not seem to work, simply change the plan without changing your goal. If you make this principle a part of your life, you will be able to achieve most of your life's goals.

POSSESS A BEGINNER'S MIND

A common problem when a group of experts get together is that they can all think they have the right answer. Bezos prefers to view things with a "beginner's mind." By adopting this student mentality, innovation and fresh ideas are encouraged instead of being held back by outdated and overused beliefs. Additionally, you're not concerned by how others view you, rather, you're focused on growth. That gives you the liberty to pursue bias for action, to experiment and make mistakes. To experiment and succeed.

FOREVER EVOLVE

Bezos took his mantra, "What's dangerous is not to evolve" and applied it to his leadership when he bought *The Washington Post* in 2013. The publication, while old school and respected, had long been failing in terms of readership and expansion.

Two points of evolution for this endeavor? He's already increased web traffic growth and brought new ideas.

The first is in part due to him integrating aggregation content into the site. Bezos did so after seeing that aggregator sites were getting more traffic by summing up articles from the *Post* than the publication got writing them.

As for ideas, Bezos gave funding to *PostEverything*, a millennial-focused site for experts to publish their opinions.

He is also trying an experiment where in lieu of running costly global news bureaus, he's instituted an automated web hub that connects *The Post* to hundreds of freelancers in the U.S. who can be assigned articles.

Will it work? Let's be like Bezos and see.

FOLLOW THE TWO PIZZA RULE

The two pizza rule is a bit of wisdom to keep meetings efficient. Basically, Bezos will only hold meetings in which two pizzas will feed the group. If the group that's gathered together to meet is too large, then nothing will get done. This is the most delicious solution to the problem, wouldn't you agree?

Chapter Six: Little Known Facts

"Work hard, have fun, make history."—
Jeff Bezos

THE WORLD'S CRAZIEST CLOCK

With the enormous wealth that Bezos has at his disposal, he can do pretty much anything that takes his fancy. A good example of this is investing $42 million into a mechanical clock. Not just any clock though, buried 500 feet under the peak of a mountain in Texas, a group of engineers are constructing a clock that will last 10,000 years. While very impressive, it should be noted that the clock only ticks once a century!

SLEEP IS IMPORTANT

Unlike the sleep-less nights often portrayed in todays motivational videos, advising us to 'grind all day and night,' Bezos realizes the importance of rest and recuperation. He always aims for the recommended 8 hours of sleep a night and requires no alarm clock to wake him.

FAVORITE BOOK

As you would expect from the man who owns the largest bookstore company in the world, Bezos loves to read. His favorite novel is "The Remains of the Day" written by Kazuo Ishiguro.

FIRST BOOK SOLD

The first book Amazon ever sold was called Fluid Concepts and Creative Analogies by Doug Hofstadte. This complex science book, which explores the mechanisms of intelligence through computer modelling, was sold on April 3, 1995.

CUSTOMER SATISFACTION

Running one of the most successful companies in the world is busy work and you would expect it to be near on impossible to get in touch with the guy. It's actually much easier than you would expect, Bezos has made his email address public so customers can email him directly in the case of a problem. He simply forwards the email to the relevant person with "?" and then they have to explain why the problem was there in the first place. Try your luck – jeff@amazon.com.

NEAR DEATH

2003 nearly saw the end to the amazon CEO due to a helicopter crash. Luckily Bezos walked away relatively unscathed but has never ridden in one since!

SAFETY FIRST

Jeff Bezos really doesn't want to die. He invests $1.6 million a year on personal security guards to protect him and his loved ones. According to Chris Pine he once paid a visit to the Star Trek Beyond set with nine individual guards and three limos!

STAR TREK FAN

Bezos is a huge Star Trek fan. The AI virtual assistant Alexa is inspired from the show and he once even considered renaming Amazon to MakeItSo.com after Captain Picard's catchphrase.

ONE CLICK

Amazon's famous "One Click" that allows customers to purchase goods with a single click of the mouse is a patented and trademarked operation. Apple also offers "One Click" for purchasers and is able to do so through a licensing agreement with Amazon. This means that even while consumers are using Apple products, Bezos is still getting paid.

MUSEUM HOME

Bezos currently owns a home that was previously used as a textile museum in Medina, Washington. It is now worth over $25 million.

THE INVESTOR

Bezos Expeditions, his investment fund, have made a few smart investments over the years. Notable companies include Uber, AirBnB and ZocDoc. However, the winning investment came in 1998 when Bezos invested $250,000 into a little internet search engine named Google. Today that investment is worth $3.1 billion.

SUCCESSFUL ALUMNI

Bezos obviously has an eye for recruiting bright minds with many of his former top employees leaving Amazon to build their own successful company. These include Charlie Cheever, who started Quora; Marc Lore, who started Jet.com; and Jason Kilar, who founded Hulu.

POWER HUNGRY

During Amazon's infancy out of Bezos' garage, the computer servers required to run the company used so much power that even plugging in a hair dryer would likely blow a fuse. While I'm sure this was a sacrifice to his wife at the time, it has certainly paid off!

THE $23 MILLION BOOK

Amazon once listed a book for over $23 million. What is this amazing book about I hear you ask? The genetic makeup of flies. This insane price was the result of an automatic algorithm glitch that listed the price relative to the cost of another Amazon source store. Each store's algorithm began a price war with the mistake eventually being spotted at exactly $23,698,655.93. The book was then reduced down to the correct, but still rather high, price of $106.23.

PHILANTHROPY

Over the years Bezos Expeditions has donated over $45 million to a variety of philanthropic causes. Around $25 million was pledged towards the Fred Hutchinson Cancer Research Center to aid combatting cancer. A further $20 million was donated toward various education projects including a center for innovation in Seattle and the research of neural dynamics at Princeton University.

Final Words

The life of Amazon founder and CEO Jeff Bezos is quite a story. From taking his crib apart using a screwdriver at the age of three, to building a company that has become the world's largest online retailer, and now to working on projects that might define the next step of human evolution – conquering space. In all these pursuits, Bezos has been driven by three major values: a long term view of life, steadfast determination to follow through with his vision and an experimental approach to everything.

It is my hope that this book has given you a glimpse into what it takes to become the richest person in the history of the world. I also hope that this book has inspired you to follow through with your dreams and live your best life.

Finally, I'd like to ask a small favor of you to take a minute to leave your honest feedback for this book. Your feedback will be greatly appreciated, and will help me keep producing these books for you and other readers. Thanks for reading.

Made in the USA
Coppell, TX
11 February 2022

73394616R00038